Billie Swint '01

Moosewood
Cookbook
Classics

Moosewood Cookbook Classics

by Mollie Katzen

RUNNING PRESS
PHILADELPHIA · LONDON

A Running Press Miniature Edition™
Copyright © 1977, 1992, 1996 Mollie Katzen.
Recipes in this Miniature Edition™ were originally published in Moosewood Cookbook. Reprinted by permission of Ten Speed Press.

Printed in China.

Library of Congress Cataloging-in-Publication Number 96-67131
ISBN 1-56138-775-4

This book may be ordered by mail from the publisher. Please include $1.00 for postage and handling. But try your bookstore first!
Running Press Book Publishers
125 South Twenty-second Street
Philadelphia, Pennsylvania 19103-4399

Contents

Tabouli 37

White Rabbit Salad 40

Bermuda Salad 41

Marinated Sweet Potatoes

    & Broccoli 45

SAUCES AND DIPS

Eggplant Scallopini

Marsala 50

Salsa Fresca 54

Zingy Bean Dip 61

ENTRÉES

Broccoli Mushroom Noodle

    Casserole 66

DESSERTS

Preface

In the early 1970s, I went to visit my brother and some friends in upstate New York. They were about to start a restaurant, and I ended up staying to help create and open the business.

We named the restaurant "Moosewood," after a local variety of maple tree, and before I knew it, my visit to the area had turned into a five-year commitment. During that time I kept journals of recipes for the original dishes we prepared in our ever evolving vegetarian kitchen. When customers asked for recipes, I just jotted something down on a napkin or any handy scrap of paper.

Eventually, I collected the recipes into a small, casual, hand-lettered and illustrated cookbook, both for my use in the kitchen and for our customers' use at home. With a loan from a local bookstore, I printed 800 copies of the Moosewood Cookbook. To my astonishment, it sold out in two weeks. A second printing of 2,000 copies also vanished in short order.

The audience for Moosewood's easy-to-prepare, ethnically influenced, meatless dishes turned out to be far wider than anyone anticipated. Twenty years and more than two million copies later I'm still amazed by the enthusiasm with which the Moosewood recipes have been received.

My cooking has evolved over the years. My dishes are now lower in fat, dairy, and egg content, and more intense in seasoning and color. The Moosewood Cookbook, which has been revised to keep pace, focuses more than ever on fresh ingredients and a healthful way of eating.

It's been a great privilege for me to have contributed to the growing interest in wholesome, healthy food among both meat eaters and vegetarians. I hope this sampling of some of my favorite recipes will bring you much pleasure.

SOUPS

Gypsy Soup

Preparation time:
about 45 minutes

Yield:
4 to 5 servings

...a delicately spiced Spanish-style
vegetable soup...

The vegetables in this soup can be varied. Any orange vegetable can be combined with any green. For example, peas or green beans could replace—or—augment the peppers. Carrots, pumpkin, or squash could fill in for the sweet potatoes. Innovate!

NOTE: Chick peas need to be cooked in advance. (canned = OK)

Gypsy Soup

2 medium-sized ripe
   tomatoes
2 Tbs. olive oil
2 cups chopped onion
3 medium cloves garlic,
   crushed
1 stalk celery, minced
2 cups peeled, diced
   sweet potato
1 tsp. salt
2 tsp. mild paprika

1 tsp. turmeric
1 tsp. basil
a dash of cinnamon
a dash of cayenne
1 bay leaf
3 cups water
1 medium bell pepper,
   diced
1 1/2 cups cooked
   chick peas

1) Heat a medium-sized saucepanful of
water to boiling. Core the tomatoes, and
plunge them into the boiling water for a
slow count of 10. Remove the tomatoes,

and peel them over a sink. Cut them open;
squeeze out and discard the seeds. Chop
the remaining pulp and set aside.

2) Heat the olive oil in a kettle or Dutch
oven. Add onion, garlic, celery, and sweet
potato, and sauté over medium heat for
about 5 minutes. Add salt, and sauté 5
minutes more. Add seasonings and water,
cover, and simmer about 15 minutes.

3) Add tomato pulp, bell pepper, and chick
peas. Cover and simmer for about 10 more
minutes, or until all the vegetables are as
tender as you like them. Taste to adjust
seasonings, and serve.

Cream of Broccoli

Preparation time:
about 45 minutes

Yield:
4 to 6 servings

2 Tbs. butter or
   margarine
1 1/2 cups chopped onion
1 bay leaf
1 tsp. salt (more, to
   taste)
1 medium bell pepper,
   diced
4 cups chopped broccoli
2 1/2 cups water

2 cups milk (lowfat OK)
1/2 cup sour cream
   (lowfat OK)
1/4 tsp. allspice
black pepper (to taste)
white pepper (to taste)
a dash of thyme
1/2 tsp. basil
1 cup broccoli florets,
   sliced thin and
   lightly steamed

1) Melt butter or margarine in a kettle or Dutch oven. Add onion, bay leaf, and salt. Sauté over medium heat until the onion is translucent.

2) Add green pepper, chopped broccoli, and water. Cover, and cook over medium heat for 10 minutes, or until the broccoli is very tender.

3) Remove the bay leaf, and purée the soup little by little with the milk in a blender or food processor.

4) Whisk in the sour cream and remaining seasonings. Heat gently. Serve hot, topped with lightly steamed broccoli florets.

Split Pea Soup

Preparation time:
1 hour

Yield:
6 servings or more

Instead of sautéing the vegetables, you add them directly to the simmering soup. Thus, with the exception of the optional sesame oil garnish, this soup is fat-free.

3 cups dry split peas
about 7 cups of water
   (more, as needed)
1 bay leaf

2 tsp. salt
½ to 1 tsp. dry
   mustard
2 cups minced onion

4 to 5 medium cloves
    garlic, crushed

3 stalks celery, minced

2 medium carrots,
    sliced or diced

1 small potato,
    thinly sliced

lots of freshly ground
    black pepper

3 to 4 Tbs. red wine
    vinegar (to taste)

TOPPINGS

Chinese sesame oil
    (optional)

a fresh, ripe tomato,
    diced

freshly minced parsley

1) Place split peas, water, bay leaf, salt,
and dry mustard in a kettle or Dutch
oven. Bring to a boil, lower heat as much
as possible, and simmer, partially covered,
for about 20 minutes.

2) Add onion, garlic, celery, carrots, and potato. Partially cover, and leave it to simmer gently for about 40 more minutes with occasional stirring. If necessary, add some water.

3) Add black pepper and vinegar to taste. Serve topped with a drizzle of sesame oil, diced tomato, and minced parsley.

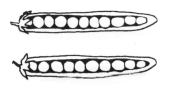

Mushroom–Barley Soup

Preparation time:
1 1/4 hours

Yield:
6 to 8 servings

1/2 cup uncooked pearl
   barley
6 1/2 cups water
1 to 2 Tbs. butter
1 medium onion,
   chopped (about
   1 1/2 cups)

2 medium cloves garlic,
   minced
1 lb. mushrooms, sliced
1/2 to 1 tsp. salt
3 to 4 Tbs. soy sauce
3 to 4 Tbs. dry sherry
freshly ground black
   pepper

1) Place the barley and 1 1/2 cups of the
water in a large saucepan or a Dutch oven.

Bring to a boil, cover, and simmer until the barley is tender (20 to 30 minutes).

2) Meanwhile, melt the butter in a skillet. Add the onions and sauté for about 5 minutes over medium heat. Add garlic, mushrooms, and $\frac{1}{2}$ tsp. salt. Cover and cook, stirring occasionally, until everything is very tender—about 10 to 12 minutes. Stir in soy sauce and sherry.

3) Add the sauté with all its liquid to the cooked barley, along with the remaining 5

cups of water. Grind in a generous amount of black pepper, and simmer, partially covered, another 20 minutes over very low heat. Taste to correct seasonings, and serve.

Chilled Cucumber-Yogurt Soup

Preparation time:
less than 10 minutes, plus
time to chill

Yield:
4 to 6 servings

4 cups peeled, seeded,
    & grated cucumber
2 cups water
2 cups yogurt
    (nonfat OK)
½ to 1 tsp. salt

1 small clove garlic,
    minced
1 tsp. dried dill (or
    1 Tbs. fresh)
1 Tbs. honey (optional)
    minced fresh mint
    and chives

Combine grated cucumber, water, yogurt, salt, garlic, dill, and optional honey in a medium-sized bowl. Stir until well blended, and chill until very cold. Serve topped with finely minced fresh herbs, if available.

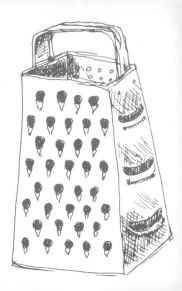

Salads

Warm Salad

...featuring an assortment of ultranutritious leafy greens, lightly cooked and delicately marinated. This can be a main dish unto itself, or a prelude or accompaniment to a simple pasta supper. However you serve it, be sure to include some fresh crusty bread to mop up the juices.

NOTE: Other types of greens can be substituted for the escarole, chard, and mustard. Try kale, collard, or dandelion greens.

Warm Salad

3 Tbs. olive oil
1 small bunch escarole,
    chopped
1 medium bunch red or
    green chard, chopped
about 8 large leaves Napa
    or Savoy cabbage,
    chopped
2 cups (packed) chopped
    mustard greens
1 to 2 tsp. salt

2 large cloves garlic,
    minced
2 medium leeks, chopped
2 cups chopped red onion
³⁄₄ lb. mushrooms, sliced
1 stalk celery, sliced
¹⁄₂ small cauliflower,
    chopped
3 Tbs. balsamic or wine
    vinegar
6 Tbs. (or more) parmesan
lots of fresh black pepper

1) Heat 1 Tbs. olive oil in a large wok or
deep skillet. Add the escarole, chard,
cabbage, and mustard greens, a little

at a time, salting lightly after each
addition, and adding more greens as soon
as the ones in the pot cook down enough
to make room. Use a fairly intense level of
heat under the pot, and stir as you cook.
When all the greens are wilted and tender, stir in the garlic. Cook and stir just
a minute or two more, then transfer to
a platter.

2) Add the remaining oil to the wok or
skillet, and when it is hot, add leeks,
onion, mushrooms, celery, and cauliflower.
Salt lightly, and stir-fry quickly over
medium-high heat until just tender

(about 5 to 8 minutes). Add to the platter, mix gently to incorporate the greens,
and sprinkle with vinegar and parmesan
while still hot. Grind black pepper over
the top, and serve hot, warm, or at room
temperature, with thick slices of toasted
bread to mop up the juices. (Sourdough
bread is especially good for this.)

Macedonian Salad

Preparation time:
40 minutes,
plus time to marinate

Yield:
4 to 6 servings
(possibly more depending
on the context)

...small cubes of roasted eggplant, marinated with fresh vegetables in a lemony, herby vinaigrette

TIME SAVER: Prepare other things while the eggplant cooks.

1 large eggplant (about 9 inches long)—or its approximate equivalent in medium or small eggplants —peeled or not, and cut into 1-inch cubes, or even smaller a little oil, for the baking tray

Macedonian Salad

- 4 Tbs. olive oil
- 2 Tbs. red wine vinegar
- 1 medium clove garlic, minced
- 1/2 tsp. salt (more, to taste)
- freshly ground black pepper
- 1/2 tsp. basil
- 1/4 tsp. thyme
- 1/4 tsp. marjoram or oregano
- 1 Tbs. fresh lemon juice
- 1/4 cup (packed) finely minced parsley
- 2 small scallions, very finely minced
- 1/2 medium red bell pepper, minced
- 1/2 medium green bell pepper, minced
- 1 medium tomato, diced

OPTIONAL GARNISHES:
- olives (Greek, oil-cured, or Niçoise)
- yogurt
- crumbled feta cheese

1) Preheat oven to 375°F. Spread the eggplant cubes onto a lightly oiled baking

tray, and roast in the oven about 15 minutes, or until tender enough so a fork can slide in easily. Remove from oven.

2) Meanwhile, combine the olive oil, vinegar, garlic, salt, pepper, herbs, and lemon juice in a medium-sized bowl. Add the still-warm eggplant and stir. Cover, and let sit for at least 2 hours. (At this stage, it will keep in the refrigerator for several days.)

3) Add the remaining vegetables within an hour or two of serving. Serve garnished with olives and yogurt or crumbled feta cheese.

Tabouli

Preparation time:
30 to 40 minutes

Yield:
6 to 8 servings

...the classic bulgur salad with garlic, parsley, lemon, mint, etc.

You can prepare Steps 1 and 2 as much as a day or two in advance. The flavors get deeper as it sits around. A food processor does a perfect job of mincing scallions, parsley, and mint into a fine feathery state, which makes the salad much prettier and easier to eat.

1 cup dry bulgur wheat
1 $\frac{1}{2}$ cups boiling water
1 to 1 $\frac{1}{2}$ tsp. salt
$\frac{1}{4}$ cup fresh lemon juice
$\frac{1}{4}$ cup olive oil
2 medium cloves garlic, crushed
black pepper, to taste
4 scallions, finely minced (whites and greens)
1 packed cup minced parsley

10 to 15 fresh mint leaves, minced (or 1 to 2 Tbs. dried mint)
2 medium-sized ripe tomatoes, diced

OPTIONAL:
$\frac{1}{2}$ cup cooked chick peas
1 medium bell pepper, diced
1 small cucumber, seeded & minced

1) Combine bulgur and boiling water in a

medium-large bowl. Cover and let stand
until the bulgur is tender (20 to 30
minutes, minimum).

2) Add salt, lemon juice, olive oil, garlic,
and black pepper, and mix thoroughly.
Cover tightly and refrigerate until about
30 minutes before serving.

3) About 30 minutes before serving,
stir in remaining ingredients (including
optional additions) and mix well. Serve
cold with warm wedges of lightly toasted
pita bread.

White Rabbit Salad

Preparation time:
15 minutes

Yield:
about 6 servings

3 cups cottage cheese
(may be lowfat)
1 to 2 Tbs. honey
(optional), to taste
2 to 3 Tbs. lemon
juice, to taste
$1/4$ cup (packed) raisins
or currants
$1/2$ cup chopped,
toasted nuts
1 Tbs. poppy seeds

2 medium-sized tart
apples, diced

PLUS MANY OPTIONS:
fresh peach slices
fresh pear slices
seedless red or green
grapes
orange sections
chunks of ripe honeydew
or cantaloupe

Combine everything and chill.

40

Bermuda Salad

Preparation time:
20 to 30 minutes,
plus time to marinate

Yield:
4 to 6 servings, depending
on what goes with it

...marinated fresh whole green beans and
onion slices with a touch of cheese...

6 Tbs. olive oil
3 to 4 Tbs. red wine
    vinegar
1 1/4 tsp. salt
2 medium cloves garlic,
    minced

fresh black pepper,
    to taste
1 1/2 cups thinly sliced
    red onion
3 cups boiling water

1 1/2 lbs. fresh green
   beans, ends trimmed
1 to 2 cups (packed)
   mild or medium
   cheddar, grated

OPTIONAL:
about 1/2 cup finely
   minced parsley

1) Combine oil, vinegar, salt, garlic, and
black pepper in a medium-sized bowl.
2) Place the sliced onion in a colander

over the sink, and slowly douse it with 3
cups boiling water. Drain thoroughly, and
transfer to the marinade, mixing well.
3) Steam the green beans until just
tender, then immediately transfer to
a colander and refresh them under cold
running water. Drain well, and add to the
marinade, along with the grated cheese
(sprinkle it in as you mix gently). You can
also throw in some finely minced parsley.
4) Marinate for at least several hours,
either refrigerated or at room temperature, stirring occasionally. Serve cold or
at room temperature.

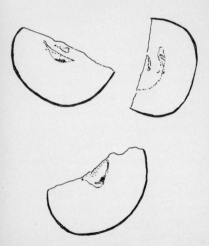

Marinated Sweet Potatoes & Broccoli

Preparation time:
15 to 20 minutes; at least
2 hours to marinate

Yield:
about 6 servings

3 medium-sized sweet
   potatoes or yams
   (1 1/2 to 2 lbs.)

MARINADE:
1/2 cup walnut oil
   (if unavailable, use
   olive oil)
1 large clove garlic,
   minced

3 Tbs. lemon juice
2 Tbs. raspberry vinegar
   (if unavailable, use red
   wine vinegar)
1 to 1 1/2 tsp. salt
1 Tbs. dry mustard
1 Tbs. honey
freshly ground black
   pepper

1 large bunch broccoli
(1 to 1 ½ lbs.), cut
into small spears

OPTIONAL GARNISHES:
thin slices of green
apple
chopped, toasted
pecans

1) Peel the sweet
potatoes, cut them
in halves or quarters,
then into thin slices. Put
them up to cook, either in or over boiling
water (in a steamer). Meanwhile, prepare
the marinade.

2) Combine the marinade ingredients in a
medium-large bowl. As soon as the sweet

potato slices are tender, add them, still hot, to the marinade. Mix gently.

3) Steam the broccoli until bright green and just tender. Rinse under cold running water and drain completely. Lay the broccoli spears carefully on top of the salad. Cover tightly and marinate for several hours.

4) Within 15 minutes of serving, mix in the broccoli from on top. Serve garnished with thin slices of green apple and chopped, toasted pecans.

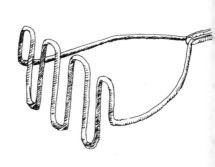

Sauces and Dips

Eggplant Scallopini Marsala

Preparation time:
45 minutes

Yield:
about 6 servings

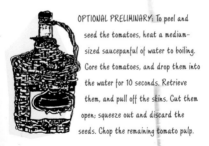

OPTIONAL PRELIMINARY: To peel and
seed the tomatoes, heat a medium-
sized saucepanful of water to boiling.
Core the tomatoes, and drop them into
the water for 10 seconds. Retrieve
them, and pull off the skins. Cut them
open; squeeze out and discard the
seeds. Chop the remaining tomato pulp.

NOTE: The alcohol content of the wine will dissipate during cooking.

2 to 3 Tbs. olive oil
2 cups chopped onion
2 bay leaves
6 cups diced eggplant (about 1 large eggplant, peeling optional)
2 medium-sized bell peppers, any color, diced
1 lb. mushrooms, chopped
2 tsp. salt
2 tsp. dried basil (or 2 Tbs. minced fresh)
1 cup marsala or dry sherry

3 to 4 medium-sized ripe tomatoes, chopped (Peeling and seeding = optional. See "optional preliminary" above.)
black pepper, to taste
8 to 10 medium cloves garlic, minced
1 lb. pasta—any shape
OPTIONAL:
additional olive oil, for the pasta
parmesan
finely minced parsley

51

1) Heat the olive oil in a deep skillet. Add onion and bay leaves, and sauté over medium heat until the onions are soft (5 to 8 minutes).

2) Add eggplant, peppers, mushrooms, salt, and basil. Cover and cook until the eggplant is tender (10 to 15 minutes), stirring occasionally.

3) Add wine, tomatoes, and black pepper. Simmer 10 to 15 minutes uncovered (the liquid will reduce). Stir in the garlic during the last 5 minutes. Meanwhile cook the pasta.

4) Drain the pasta, toss with a little additional olive oil, and ladle the eggplant on top. Sprinkle with parmesan and parsley, and serve.

Salsa Fresca

Great as a dip for chips, with any bean dish, next to omelettes, with plain rice, on top of tortillas, or in partnership with Zingy Bean Dip (p. 61) or guacamole. If you eat chicken or fish, try serving the Pineapple or Mango Salsa alongside— they make exquisite relishes.

Pineapple Salsa

Preparation time:
15 minutes (w/ fresh
pineapple) or 5 minutes
(w/ canned)

Yield:
2 cups

2 cups minced fresh
   (or canned-in-juice)
   pineapple
2 medium cloves garlic,
   minced

2 to 3 Tbs. minced
   fresh mint
2 Tbs. fresh lime juice
¼ tsp. salt
¼ tsp. cumin
cayenne, to taste

Combine everything, cover tightly, and
refrigerate. This keeps a long time.

Mango Salsa

Preparation time:
10 minutes

Yield:
1 ½ cups

2 Tbs. finely minced red onion
2 cups boiling water
1 average-sized (about 6 inches long) ripe mango (if you're lucky enough to find one) —about 1 ½ cups minced

2 Tbs. fresh lime juice
1 medium clove garlic, minced
½ tsp. salt
2 Tbs. minced fresh cilantro
OPTIONAL:
cayenne, to taste

Mango Salsa

Place the minced onion in a small strainer
over a bowl. Slowly pour the boiling water
over the onion, then let it sit for 5 minutes. This will soften its bite, and turn
it a striking shade of purple-pink.
Combine all ingredients and mix gently.
Cover tightly and refrigerate.

Tomato Salsa

Preparation time:
10 minutes

Yield:
1 ½ to 2 cups

3 medium-sized ripe
 tomatoes
2 scallions, finely
 minced
2 medium cloves garlic,
 minced
a handful of parsley,
 finely minced
a handful of cilantro,
 finely minced

1 tsp. lightly toasted
 cumin seeds
³⁄₄ to 1 tsp. salt
1 Tbs. cider vinegar
1 Tbs. olive oil
1 Tbs. fresh lime juice
 crushed red pepper,
 to taste

Drop the tomatoes into a potful of simmering water for 10 seconds. Take them
out, pull off the skins, and squeeze out
the seeds. Dice the remaining pulp.
Combine everything in a small bowl or
container. Cover tightly and chill.

NOTE: To toast the cumin seeds, use
a small skillet over a low flame or
a toaster oven. With either
method, watch them
carefully so they won't
scorch.

Zingy Bean Dip

Preparation time:
less than 10 minutes

Yield:
about 2 cups

It's hard to find anything new to say in
the Bean Dip Department, but this one
gets a few words in.

Canned pinto beans work so well in here
that I encourage you to use them. Be
sure to rinse and drain them well. If you
also use a food processor, this recipe will
be very quick.

Serve it with chips, vegetables, crack-
ers, or warmed flour tortillas. Pair it with

any Salsa Fresca (p. 54) for some serious appetizer activity.

To peel and seed a tomato: Drop it into a pan of boiling water for 10 seconds. Remove it, and peel off the skin. Cut the tomato open; squeeze out and discard the seeds. Chop the remaining pulp.

2 cups cooked pinto beans
(1 15-oz. can), rinsed
and well drained
2 Tbs. fresh lime juice
1 medium-sized tomato,
peeled and seeded
(see above)

1 to 2 medium cloves
garlic, minced
a handful of parsley
a handful of cilantro
$3/4$ tsp. cumin
OPTIONAL:
1 scallion, minced

$1/4$ to $1/2$ tsp. salt   black pepper and
                           cayenne, to taste

Whip it all up together in a food processor
or a blender.

Entrées

Broccoli Mushroom Noodle Casserole

Preparation time:
30 minutes;
45 minutes to bake

Yield:
about 6 servings

1 1-lb. (or 12-oz.)
package wide flat
egg noodles
2 Tbs. butter or
margarine
2 cups chopped onion
3 medium cloves garlic,
minced

1 large bunch fresh
broccoli, chopped
1 lb. mushrooms, sliced
or chopped
1/2 tsp. salt (more, to
taste)
lots of fresh black
pepper

OPTIONAL: ¼ cup dry
    white wine
OPTIONAL: 3 eggs,
    beaten
3 cups (1 ½ lbs.)
    cottage cheese (may be
    lowfat)
1 cup sour cream (may be
    lowfat) or buttermilk

1 ½ cups fine bread
    crumbs and/or
    wheat germ
OPTIONAL: 1 cup
    (packed) grated
    medium or sharp
    cheddar

1) Preheat oven to 350°F. Butter or oil
a 9 x 13-inch baking pan.
2) Cook the noodles in plenty of boiling
water until about half-done. Drain and

rinse under cold water. Drain again and
set aside.

3) Melt the butter or margarine in a large
skillet, and add onions and garlic. Sauté
for about 5 minutes over medium heat,
then add broccoli, mushrooms, salt, and
pepper. Continue to cook, stirring frequently, until the broccoli is bright green
and just tender. Remove from heat and
possibly add optional white wine.

4) In a large bowl, beat together optional eggs (or not) with cottage cheese and sour cream or buttermilk. Add noodles, sautéed vegetables, and 1 cup of the bread crumbs. Mix well.

5) Spread into the prepared pan, and top with remaining bread crumbs and, if desired, grated cheese. Bake covered for 30 minutes; uncovered for 15 minutes more.

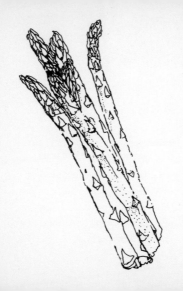

Tart & Tangy Baked Beans

Preparation time:
Presoaked beans need up
to 1 ½ hours to cook.
Get everything else ready
during this time.

Yield:
6 to 8 servings

A version of this recipe appeared in early editions of the Moosewood Cookbook as "Cheese Beans." This one is more deeply seasoned, but basically the same. Cheese is optional.

Serve this with rice, corn bread, or warmed tortillas.

NOTE: The beans need to soak for at least 4 hours ahead of time.

3 cups dry pinto beans, soaked

4 cups chopped onions

2 Tbs. olive oil

1 1/2 to 2 tsp. salt

1 Tbs. chili powder

2 tsp. cumin

1 1/2 tsp. dry mustard

6 to 8 medium cloves garlic, minced

6 Tbs. dry white wine (optional)

6 to 8 Tbs. cider vinegar (to taste)

3 to 4 Tbs. molasses (to taste)

2 cups grated mild cheese (optional)

lots of black pepper

crushed red pepper, to taste

3 medium-sized tart apples, cut into medium-sized chunks

4 medium-sized ripe tomatoes, chopped

Tart & Tangy Baked Beans

1) Place the presoaked beans in a kettle and cover them with plenty of water. Bring to a boil, lower to a simmer, partially cover, and cook slowly until tender (1 1/4 to 1 1/2 hours), checking the water level during cooking. Drain off any excess when the beans are done. (This can be saved for soup stock.)

2) Begin cooking the onions in olive oil in a medium-sized skillet. Add salt, chili powder, cumin, and mustard, and sauté over medium heat for about 8 to 10 minutes. Add garlic, and sauté for another 5 minutes or so. Add this sauté to the cooked

73

beans, along with all remaining ingredients.
3) Preheat oven to 350°F. Mix the beans
well and transfer to a deep casserole or a
9 x 13-inch baking pan. Cover tightly with
foil, and bake 1 hour.

Arabian Squash Casserole

Preparation time:
about 1 hour, after the
squash is cooked and puréed.

Yield:
4 to 5 servings

Good served with Tabouli Salad (p. 37),
or with warmed pita bread and a spinach
salad with ripe tomatoes.

PRELIMINARY: Preheat oven to 375°F.

4 cups cooked squash
    or pumpkin, mashed
    or puréed
1 Tbs. olive oil
1 ½ cups chopped onion

1 tsp. salt
2 small bell peppers
    (one red and one
    green, if possible),
    minced

4 or 5 medium cloves
    garlic, minced
black pepper and
    cayenne, to taste
1/2 cup firm yogurt

1 cup crumbled feta
    cheese
OPTIONAL: sunflower
    seeds and/or minced
    walnuts, for the top

1) Place the mashed or puréed squash in a large bowl.

2) Heat the olive oil in a medium-sized skillet. Add onion, and sauté over medium heat for about 5 minutes. Add salt and bell peppers. Sauté about 5 more minutes, or until the peppers begin to get soft.

3) Add garlic, black pepper, and cayenne, and sauté a few more minutes.

4) Add the sauté, along with yogurt and feta, to the squash, and mix well. Spread into an ungreased 9-inch square baking pan; sprinkle the top lightly with sun- flower seeds and/or minced walnuts.
5) Bake uncovered for 25 to 30 minutes, or until bubbly.

Chilean Squash
(a variation)

Delete: yogurt, feta, sunflower seeds, walnuts.

Add to step 2: 1 tsp. cumin, $\frac{1}{2}$ tsp. dried coriander (optional), 1 tsp. chili powder, 2 cups corn (frozen/defrosted = OK)

Top with: 1 cup grated cheddar

Zucchini-Feta Pancakes

Preparation time:
30 minutes

Yield:
serves about 4

...Light and very satisfying (also quite attractive, with lovely flecks of green). A food processor will grate the zucchini in seconds flat.

NOTE: This recipe calls for 4 eggs. Some or all of the yolks can be deleted.

4 eggs, separated
    (yolks optional)

4 packed cups coarsely
    grated zucchini (about
    4 7-inchers)

1 cup finely crumbled
   feta cheese
½ cup finely minced
   scallions
1 tsp. dried mint (or
   1 Tbs. fresh, finely
   minced)

a little salt (optional,
   to taste)
lots of black pepper
⅓ cup flour
oil for frying
sour cream or yogurt
   for topping

1) Beat the egg whites until stiff.
2) In a medium-sized bowl, combine zucchini, egg yolks (or not), feta, scallions, seasonings, and flour. Mix well.
3) Fold the egg whites into the zucchini mixture.
4) Heat a little oil in a heavy skillet.

When it is very hot, add spoonfuls of batter, and fry on both sides until golden and crisp.

5) Serve immediately, topped with sour cream or yogurt.

Spinach-Ricotta Pie

Preparation time:
40 minutes; 40 to 45
more to bake

Yield:
4 to 6 servings

THE CRUST:
6 Tbs. butter or
    margarine, cut into
    small pieces
1 1/2 cups flour
about 4 Tbs. cold water,
    milk, or buttermilk

THE FILLING:
1 tsp. butter or
    margarine

1 cup minced onion
1 lb. spinach, stemmed
    and finely chopped
1/2 tsp. salt
freshly ground pepper,
    to taste
1 tsp. basil
1 lb. ricotta cheese
2 or 3 beaten eggs
3 Tbs. flour

½ cup (packed) grated
    sharp cheese of your
    choice
a dash of nutmeg
    (optional)

OPTIONAL TOPPING:
1 cup sour cream (may
    be lowfat), lightly
    beaten
paprika

CRUST:

1) Use a pastry cutter, two forks, or a food processor to cut together the butter and flour until the mixture is uniformly blended and resembles coarse cornmeal. (The food processor will do this in just a few spurts.)

2) Add just enough liquid (water, milk, or buttermilk) to hold the dough together.

Roll out the dough and form a crust in a 9- or 10-inch pie pan. Set aside.

FILLING:

3) Preheat oven to 375°F. Melt the butter or margarine in a medium-sized skillet, add the onion, and sauté for 5 minutes over medium heat. Add spinach, salt, pepper, and basil, and cook, stirring, over medium-high heat until the spinach is wilted. Remove from heat.

4) Combine all filling ingredients in a large bowl, and mix well. Spread into the

unbaked pie shell. For an
extra rich pie, top with
sour cream, spread to
the edges of the crust.
Dust generously with
paprika.

5) Bake 40 to
45 minutes, or
until firm to
the touch at
the center. Serve
hot, warm, or at
room temperature.

Eggplant Curry

Preparation time:
45 minutes (put up
rice when you begin)

Yield:
6 to 8 servings

2 to 3 Tbs. butter
   and/or peanut oil
1 Tbs. mustard seeds
2 Tbs. sesame seeds
2 tsp. cumin seeds
1 1/2 cups chopped onion
1 1/2 to 2 tsp. salt
2 tsp. turmeric
1/4 tsp. cayenne (possibly
   more, depending on
   your tolerance
   preference)

2 medium eggplants
   (7 to 8 inches long;
   4-inch diameter at
   roundest point), cut
   into 1-inch cubes
water, as needed
2 cups frozen or fresh
   green peas

OPTIONAL:
1 small bunch fresh
   cilantro, minced

1) Heat butter or oil over medium heat in a very large, deep skillet or Dutch oven. Add seeds, and sauté until they begin to pop (5 minutes).

2) Add onion, salt, turmeric, and cayenne. Cook, stirring occasionally, for 8 to 10 minutes, or until the onion is translucent.

3) Add eggplant and salt. Cook, stirring from the bottom regularly, for 15 to 20 minutes—until the eggplant is soft.

You might need to add a little water if the mixture is too dry. Cover the pan between stirrings.

4) Steam the peas until they are just tender and bright green. Serve the curry over rice, topped with peas and freshly minced cilantro.

Vegetable Stew

Preparation time:
about 50 minutes

Yield:
about 6 servings

2 Tbs. olive oil and/or
   butter
3 cups minced onion
3 medium cloves garlic,
   minced
2 medium potatoes,
   diced

1 medium (7-inch or so)
   eggplant, diced
1 tsp. salt (more, to
   taste)
fresh black pepper, to
   taste

Vegetable Stew

2 medium stalks celery, chopped

1 healthy stalk broccoli, chopped small

2 to 3 medium carrots, sliced or diced

½ cup dry red wine (optional)

2 small (6-inch) zucchini, diced

3 Tbs. (half a small can) tomato paste

½ lb. mushrooms, coarsely chopped

3 Tbs. molasses

2 tsp. dill

OPTIONAL TOPPINGS:
sour cream or yogurt
finely minced parsley

1) Heat oil (or melt butter) in a Dutch oven. Add onion, garlic, potatoes, eggplant, salt, and pepper. Cover and cook over medium heat, stirring often, until the potatoes are tender. Add small amounts of water, as needed, to prevent sticking.

2) Add celery, broccoli, and carrots, along with optional red wine. Continue to cook over medium heat, covered but occasionally stirring, until all the vegetables begin to be tender (8 to 10 minutes).

3) Add remaining ingredients (except toppings) and stir. Cover and simmer very

quietly about 15 minutes more, stirring every once in a while. Taste to correct seasonings.

Serve piping hot, topped with sour cream or yogurt and minced parsley.

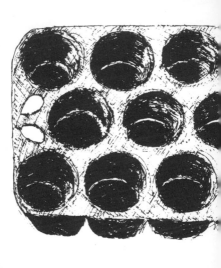

Desserts

Maple-Walnut Pie

Preparation time:
20 minutes;
30 minutes to bake

Yield:
about 6 servings

Delicious and very easy!

4 large eggs
$^3/_4$ cup real maple syrup
2 Tbs. lemon juice
$^1/_4$ to $^1/_2$ tsp. cinnamon
(to taste)
1 $^1/_2$ tsp. vanilla
extract
$^1/_4$ tsp. salt

2 cups chopped
walnuts
1 unbaked 9-inch pie
crust (p. 82)

OPTIONAL:
whipped cream, for the
top

1) Preheat oven to 375°F.

2) Beat together all ingredients, except walnuts and pie crust, until light and frothy.

3) Spread the walnuts into the unbaked crust. Pour in the batter.

4) Bake for 30 minutes or until solid in the center. Remove from oven and allow to cool for at least 30 minutes before serving.

5) Serve warm, at room temperature, or cold, with or without whipped cream.

Moosewood Fudge Brownies

Preparation time:
15 minutes;
25 minutes to bake

Yield:
a 9 X 13-inch panful

On a brownie-intensity scale of 1 to 10, these are about an 11; in other words, not for the faint-hearted. You should probably have some good vanilla or coffee ice cream on hand, or you'll find yourself running out to the store to get some as soon as you take a bite, and this will rudely interrupt your dessert hour.

butter for the pan

5 oz. (5 squares) un-
sweetened chocolate

$\frac{1}{2}$ lb. (2 sticks) butter or
margarine, softened

1 $\frac{3}{4}$ cups (packed) light
brown sugar (white
sugar also OK)

5 eggs

1 $\frac{1}{2}$ tsp. vanilla
extract

1 cup flour (use $\frac{3}{4}$ cup
for fudgier brownies)

MANY OPTIONAL
EMBELLISHMENTS:

1 cup chopped walnuts
or pecans

1 tsp. freshly grated
orange rind

$\frac{1}{2}$ tsp. cinnamon

a small ripe banana,
mashed

2 to 4 Tbs. strong
black coffee

1 cup semisweet
chocolate chips

OR anything else you
might think of

OR, for purists, none of
the above

1) Butter a 9 x 13-inch baking pan.
Preheat oven to 350°F.

2) Gently melt the chocolate. Let it cool
for about 10 minutes.

3) Cream the butter and sugar in a
medium-sized bowl until light and fluffy.

4) Add the eggs, one at a time, beating
well after each. Stir in the vanilla.

5) Stir constantly as you drizzle in the
melted chocolate. After all the chocolate
is in, beat well for a minute or two.

6) Stir in flour and possible embellishments. Mix just enough to blend
thoroughly.

7) Spread the batter into the prepared pan. Bake 20 to 25 minutes, or until a knife inserted into the center comes out clean. Cut into squares while still hot, then allow to cool for at least 10 minutes, if you can wait that long.

Lemon Mousse

Preparation time:
1 hour, plus time to
chill

Yield:
6 servings

Ethereal, yet it packs a tangy punch.
Lemon Mousse will keep well for several
days if tightly covered and refrigerated.

¼ cup cornstarch

½ cup sugar

½ cup freshly squeezed
lemon juice

¹½ cup water
1 tsp. grated lemon rind
2 egg whites, at room
    temperature
¹½ pint heavy cream

OPTIONAL VARIATIONS:
1 cup berries or sliced
    peaches
orange rind, instead of
    lemon

1) Place cornstarch and sugar in a small saucepan. Add lemon juice and water and whisk until smooth.

2) Cook, whisking constantly, over medium heat until thick (5 to 8 minutes). Remove from heat, transfer to a medium-sized

bowl, and stir in the lemon rind. Let cool to room temperature.

3) Place the egg whites in a medium-sized mixing bowl and beat at high speed with an electric mixer until stiff but not dry. Fold this into the lemon mixture, cover tightly, and chill at least 1 hour (longer = also OK).

4) Without cleaning the beaters, whip the cream until it is firm but still fluffy. Fold this into the mousse (add optional berries or peaches at this point), cover tightly again, and chill until serving time.

Danish Cherries

Preparation time:
about 30 minutes

Yield:
about 6 servings

Make this delicious, beautiful, and very
simple stovetop dessert well in advance
OR right before serving. You can get fine
results from frozen cherries (they come
pitted and unsweetened in sealed plastic
bags), if fresh are unavailable. No need to
defrost before using.

NOTES: To blanch almonds, place them in a colander over a sink. Pour boiling water over them, and rub off the skins. Cut vertically with a sharp knife to sliver them.

To whip ricotta, beat it vigorously with a whisk, or at high speed with an electric mixer.

4 cups pitted cherries
1 1/2 Tbs. cornstarch
3 to 4 Tbs. sugar
1/4 cup lemon juice
1/2 tsp. grated lemon rind
3/4 tsp. almond extract

OPTIONAL: 1/2 cup blanched, slivered almonds
TOPPINGS (with a few blanched, slivered almonds folded in):
whipped cream or whipped ricotta cheese or plain yogurt

1) Place cherries in a heavy medium-sized saucepan, and cook over medium heat, covered, for 10 minutes.

2) Meanwhile, combine cornstarch and sugar in a small bowl. Add lemon juice and whisk until smooth. Stir this into the hot cherries, and cook over medium heat, stirring frequently, until thick (5 to 8 minutes).

3) Remove from heat and stir in lemon rind, almond extract, and slivered almonds. Serve hot, warm, room temperature, or cold, topped with whipped cream, whipped ricotta, or yogurt.

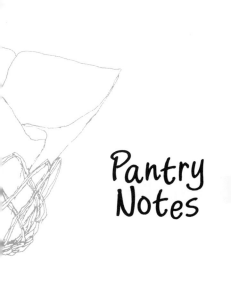

Pantry
Notes

cottage cheese, ricotta, sour cream, evaporated milk, yogurt, etc. Soy or rice milk can frequently be substituted.

EXTRACTS (VANILLA, ALMOND, ETC.): Use pure only.

FLOURS: Unless otherwise specified, use unbleached white flour.

FROZEN FOODS: I frequently tested these recipes with frozen unsweetened fruit (berries, cherries, etc.) with great success, when fresh were unavailable. You

can also use frozen peas, corn, cooked squash, and if you're in a pinch, a 10-oz. package of frozen chopped spinach can substitute for 1 large bunch fresh in cooked dishes. Defrost and drain thoroughly before using.

GARLIC: Use fresh only and buy it frequently. The fresher, the better.

HERBS: If it's not specified, the recipe was tested with dried herbs, as these are more readily available year-round. However, if you have access to fresh

herbs, by all means use them! Here's the
exchange rate: 1 tsp. dried approximately
equals 1 Tbs. minced fresh.

JUICES: Use fresh-squeezed lemon, lime,
or orange juice in these recipes whenever
possible.

OILS: For sautéing vegetables, use
peanut, corn, or pure olive oil. For salads,
use virgin or extra virgin olive oil, canola
oil, or nut oils (walnut or hazelnut). Use
virgin or extra virgin olive oil for drizzling
on pasta. For seasoning certain soups,

salads, and stir-fries, use Chinese sesame
oil (available in Asian groceries). For infor-
mation about oil sprays, see page 124.

NUTS, SEEDS, NUT BUTTERS: Use
unprocessed, available (often in bulk)
at natural foods stores and at many
grocery stores. Tahini (raw sesame paste)
is available in natural foods stores, in
some specialty groceries, and in the
imported foods section of many
grocery stores.

PASTA: The recipes in this book were

tested with dried egg pasta of various shapes, but you can also use fresh.

RICE: Short- and long-grain brown rice are interchangeable in these recipes. There is no nutritional difference, and the cooking method is the same. Short-grain is chewier; long-grain is fluffier. Buy either kind in bulk at natural foods stores.

SOY SAUCE: Japanese soy sauces (tamari or shoyu) have a deeper, slightly sweeter flavor than Chinese, which are

thinner and saltier (and sometimes contain additives, so read the label). Whichever kind you prefer, you can find good soy sauce in natural foods stores and in Asian markets.

SWEETENERS: To varying degrees, sugar, brown sugar, honey, and real maple syrup are used in the desserts. In some cases they are interchangeable. This is indicated on individual recipes.

Modifications

A brief guideline to further reduce the fat, dairy, and egg content of the recipes in this book:

LOWER-FAT COOKING:

Even though the oil content of these recipes has been pared down, you can reduce it still further by using oil sprays. These enable you to spray a mist of oil onto the food and/or the pan, instead of using oil by the tablespoon. Oil sprays are available commercially in many gourmet and natural foods stores. (The brands I know of are Pam, Bertolli, El Molino, and

Trysons.) Used in combination with high-quality nonstick cookware, oil sprays can greatly reduce the fat content of your cooking without sacrificing flavor or texture.

You can prepare your own oil sprays by filling clean, dry spray bottles with the oil of your choice. Use the type of bottle that has a nozzle that permits you to adjust the intensity of the spray, and that has an "off" position, so it won't get clogged. Store in a cool, dark cupboard.

DAIRY REDUCTION OR SUBSTITUTION:

Milk can be substituted with soy milk or rice milk, both of which are nondairy and can be found in natural foods stores.

There are some lowfat, low sodium cheeses—as well as nondairy soy cheeses—available. Be sure to taste these before using them in your cooking. They might taste perfectly fine to you, but then again, they might not. Remember, you can always cut down on the amount of cheese prescribed in a recipe and in many cases, you can omit it altogether. Whipped tofu (puréed in a blender or food

processor—or simply mashed) can sometimes substitute for cottage or ricotta
cheese in casseroles. You might want to
adjust the salt.

EGG OPTIONS:

Many of the recipes here are egg- or
yolk-optional. If you need to reduce this
further, experiment with egg substitutes.

This book has been bound using
handcraft methods, and Smyth-sewn
to ensure durability.

The dust jacket was designed by
Linda Chiu Barber
and illustrated by Mollie Katzen.

The interior was designed by
Linda Chiu Barber
and illustrated by Mollie Katzen.

The text was edited by Brian Perrin.

The text was set in Scripture.